Beekeeping

Beekeeping Guide from Beginner to Expert

Thomas Thatcher

Beekeeping

Thomas Thatcher

Contents

Page

Introduction...9
Chapter 1: Beekeeping – An Introduction................11
    Queen bee...14
    Worker bee..16
    Drones..17
    The Individual Bee..18
    Structure of hives..19
    Annual cycle of the bees...................................20
    Methods for Preventing a Swarm.....................22
    Clipping and Marking Queens..........................22
    Cutting Out Queen Cells...................................22
    Artificial Swarming...23
    The Demaree Method.......................................23

    Congestion..23
Chapter 2: Advantages of Beekeeping........................25
    Beekeeping improves crop yields..........................25
    The Importance of Pollination................................25
    You get your own stock of honey and other products..26
    Therapeutic uses..26
    Beekeeping and the Mind..27
    It is an educational hobby..28
    It is one of the most rewarding hobbies................28
Chapter 3: How to Start..31
    Are you ready to be a beekeeper?..........................31
    Source of bees...32
    Swarms...33
    Baiting..33
    Packages..33
    Nucleus Colonies..34
    Splits...35
    A beekeeper's year...35
    A beekeeper's starting kit..38
    When should I start a bee colony?........................41
Chapter 4: Taking It to the Next Level.......................43
    Hives...43
    Which beehive is the best?......................................44

Where should I put my hive?............................49

Extraction equipment.....................................52

Equipment for the winter................................54

Chapter 5: Diseases and Treatments............55

Varroa mites...55

Small hive beetles..56

Nosema..57

Wax Moths...58

Cripaviradae-Chronic Bee Paralysis Virus............58

Dicistroviridae..59

Colony Collapse Disorder..............................59

Foulbrood..61

Stonebrood..62

Iflaviridae or deformed wing virus..................63

Chapter 6: Additional Income: Starting a Small Beekeeping Operation..65

Why Beekeeping as a Business?........................65

Getting Started..68

Harvesting Cycle..70

Essential Equipment for the Small Beekeeper Operation..72

Costs..74

Additional Income: Beeswax Products 77

What is Beeswax?..77

Benefits of Beeswax in Skin Care 78
  Recipes...82
  Vitamin E Body Cream...82
  Anti-Septic Ointment...83
  Itch Relief Salve...84
  Soothing Analgesic Balm (for pain relief).............84
  Wood Conditioner..85
  Basic Beeswax Candles...85
  Nourishing Honey and Beeswax Body Soap 87
  Ingredients..87
  Supplies...88
  Additional Income Comes in Many Forms............90
Chapter 7: Some Extra Advice....................................91
  Keep a Healthy Hive...91
  Bee Stings..92
  The African honey bee...95
Conclusion..99

© Copyright 2016 BY Thomas Thatcher

All rights reserved.

In no way is it legal to reproduce, duplicate, or transmit any part of this document in either electronic means or in printed format. Recording of this publication is strictly prohibited and any storage of this document is not allowed unless with written permission from the publisher. All rights reserved.

The information provided herein is stated to be truthful and consistent, in that any liability, in terms of inattention or otherwise, by any usage or abuse of any policies, processes, or directions contained within is the solitary and utter responsibility of the recipient reader. Under no circumstances will any legal responsibility or blame be held against the publisher for any reparation, damages, or monetary loss due to the information herein, either directly or indirectly. Respective authors own all copyrights not held by the publisher.

Legal Notice:
This book is copyright protected. This is only for personal use. You cannot amend, distribute, sell, use, quote or paraphrase any part or the content within this book without the consent of the author or copyright owner. Legal action will be pursued if this is breached.

Disclaimer Notice:
Please note the information contained within this document is for educational and entertainment purposes only. Every attempt has been made to provide accurate, up to date and reliable complete information. No warranties of any kind are expressed or implied. Readers acknowledge that the author is not engaging in the rendering of legal, financial, medical or professional advice.

By reading this document, the reader agrees that under no circumstances are we responsible for any losses, direct or indirect, which are incurred as a result of the use of information contained within this document, including, but not limited to, —errors, omissions, or inaccuracies.

Thomas Thatcher

Introduction

Thank you for choosing this book.

In recent years, beekeeping has moved from an odd, obscure activity to a more ubiquitous one. Beekeeping is quickly gaining popularity as a hobby. It is fun and it encourages you spend more time in nature. Beekeeping can also be educational and teach you a great deal. If you are also someone who wants to raise bees in their backyard and make some money while you are at it, you have picked up the right book. It will help you get a better understanding of bees, how they work, how they build their hives, and much more. Beekeeping is a difficult undertaking that can be overwhelming. Reading a guide like this one is a good start. It will give you an idea of what beekeeping is like, what the possible benefits are, and the amount of time and work that is involved.

It does not matter if you do not know a single thing about beekeeping. Now is as good a time as any to start. This book begins with the assumption that you are an absolute novice in the world of beekeeping. In this book, "Beekeeping Guide: From Beginner to Expert", you will learn a lot about bees and their annual cycle. This book will also cover a lot of other topics like the common bee diseases and their treatments, and how you can take advantage of beekeeping to make good money for yourself. It will also describe the tools of the trade.

Towards the end, we will learn about extracting bee products, like honey and beeswax. We will also study different types of hives in detail. Surprisingly, there is a great deal to learn about this practice and the creatures at its center.

This guide will not only help you decide if beekeeping is something you would like to try but it will give you the basic information you need to get started. It will also serve as a reference as you work through the first year of owning a bee colony.

This book will provide you with information to consider if you are interested in making additional income from your honey production. If you soon realize that you are producing more honey and wax than you can consume, consider setting up additional hives and units, making products, such as soap, candles, skin care products, or simply sell your local, natural honey to retailers. Beekeeping is becoming more popular as a source of additional income. Many people are turning to this industry especially now as bees are becoming more and more important to the economy and continued crop growth. It is definitely the best time to start if you are interested in the beekeeping profession.

So what are you waiting for? Let's get right on to it!

# Chapter 1

Beekeeping – An Introduction

Beekeeping is also known as apiculture. It derives its name from the Latin word. "apis", which means, "bee", and as is obvious by the name, it means the maintenance of bees in colonies and hives. Beekeepers collect honey, beeswax, pollen, and other bee products by taking care of bees. Most people start beekeeping as just a hobby, and later turn it into full time work. Beekeeping has been getting a lot of attention in the recent years, and it is becoming a popular way to generate income as people's hives transition from a hobby to part of a full-fledged business. While most people can become successful beekeepers, no one can do so without gaining some important knowledge before beginning. To that end, in this chapter, we are going to discuss the basics of beekeeping and go over some general information regarding bees and beekeeping.

Beekeeping is almost as old as human civilization, dating back to nearly 13,000 BC. This early incarnation of the practice involved collecting honey from bee colonies in the wild. By 7,000 BC, people of North Africa were keeping bees in pottery vessels, and would harvest their honey. Egyptian art as old as forty-five hundred years reflects this, depicting the domestication of bees. Egyptians would float their hives down the Nile River on boats, allowing the bees to follow the bloom. In those times, the honey was stored in jars, and bees were raised in simplistic hives. While most of their craft of beekeeping was quite elementary when compared to today's, they did use smoke to control the bees, which is still common practice today.

However, it was not until the eighteenth century that people came to understand bees more deeply. Before that time, we had no understanding of their biology or how they functioned. But once we gained this insight, it allowed the development of better, more efficient methods for collecting honey. These methods were better for us and better for the bees, as they allowed a colony to survive harvesting honey. We no longer needed to destroy colonies of bees in order to harvest honey. Movable hives were an amazing development. These hives, built into wooden frames and kept together allow bees to build their hives safely, as they would in nature. They also offer beekeepers consistency and ease of access to the honey.

Today, bees travel more widely than they did in their days on the Nile. Packed on the back of large trucks, bees are shuttled around the country. They pollinate the crops of different farmers in several states, providing us with the fruits and vegetables that we eat and take for granted.

Bees have a large responsibility, and the people who care for them and facilitate their work have a great duty as well.

Some of you may have the perception that beekeeping is not complicated. This is false. Bees are some of the most hardworking beings on the planet and live in rich and complex communities. Before entering the world of apiculture, it is critical that you understand them and their world.

Aside from the production of honey, bees are perhaps best known for pollination—taking the pollen grains from one place to another and helping in the reproduction of various flora. We can thank bees for the propagation of many species of plant. In addition to that, they also produce wax; propolis, and royal jelly are a couple of other products produced by honeybees.

Bees are gregarious, social creatures that crave community. The hives are home to colonies, which have their own hierarchy. Among the bees, this hierarchy decides each bee's role in the hive. The different roles of bees have different corresponding qualities and behaviors that any beekeeper must be familiar with in order to have a working colony. There are three main classes of bees, and you need to have a healthy count of all three if you want your colony to develop properly.

Queen Bee

The Queen Bee is the only sexually active female in the hive. She has the essential task of maintaining the number of bees in the hive. During peak season, a bee colony may have as many as seventy five thousand bees. All other bees in the colony are the offspring of this queen bee. The average life span of a queen bee is about three years. In this span of three years, she will lay over half a million eggs. At the very peak of a breeding season, a queen bee may lay up to three thousand eggs every day. While such a high number is rare for a single day, you can expect at least fifteen hundred to two thousand eggs a day from a queen bee.

The queen, when she first emerges, is just like any other worker bee. She comes from a normal egg, but once she is fed a large amount of royal jelly, she becomes a queen bee. The growth of a queen into an adult is quite different from that of a normal worker bee solely because of this large amount of royal jelly.

The queen emerges from her cell after fifteen days of development. For the first three to seven days after emerging, she remains in her hive. After that, she goes out to mate. This is known as the mating flight. This is her first flight, and in this flight, she may mate with as many as fifteen drones. The subsequent flights are anywhere near five to thirty minutes long, and she mates with several male drones during each flight. Once she has collected enough sperm to fertilize a couple thousand eggs, she starts working on them.

Thomas Thatcher

Sometimes, queen bees are unable to go outside for their mating flight because of bad weather, and if they do not leave the hive for a long enough period, they become infertile. An infertile queen cannot produce more female worker bees. In some instances, the worker bees kill the infertile queen to make way for a new queen bee. They do it to increase the population of the hive, since without a fertile queen bee; the hive's population would soon dwindle and it would not survive.

Mating takes place in midair, and it is always some distance away from the hive. It is the drone's job to keep them both afloat. Strong drone bees always mate further away from the ground than weaker ones. This is a mark of their strength, and mating higher up from the ground also ensures that only the finest genes are passed to the next generation.

Once the queen bee has laid eggs, it is the job of the nurse bees to determine whether they are fertile or infertile. They also determine whether the fertile ones, all of which will be female, will develop into a worker or a queen. This will, in turn, determine the type of food they provide it during the larvae stage. It will also determine the amount of care they receive. If the nurse bees determine an egg to be a queen bee, they will build a cell resembling a small peanut around its larva. In the pupa stage, the cell is sealed and the pupa starts developing. When she has fully developed, the queen chews herself out of the shell. If she cannot, the worker bees help her get out of it.

At times, a queen bee will set out to create a new hive along with a group of some other bees. This group is referred to as a swarm. Those who are left behind raise a new queen bee to keep their hive alive.

Worker bee

All worker bees are female bees that are sexually immature. They are usually smaller in size than a queen bee. They are given less nutritious food during their twenty one days of larval and pupal development, which results in this level of development. Additionally, the queen bee suppresses the development of ovaries in other female bees living in the hive by releasing special pheromones. These worker females are, however, able to lay unfertilized eggs, which become male honey bees.

The worker bees are just what their name suggests. They do not have individual identities but instead work together toward one goal. They work around the clock to collect nectar for the improvement of the hive. They collect nectar from flowers, and this nectar is then converted into water, pollen, and honey, which are then used to feed the larvae in the hive. The worker bees also work to convert nectar into resins and gums used for coating the inside of the hive and sealing cells. They also have to take care of their queen, guard their hive, carry dead bees out of the hive, feed the young ones, and build the honey combs. The worker bees do not hesitate to lay down their lives when their hive is in danger, as they do each time they sting a possible predator. This is because they have barbed stingers, which get stuck in the victim of their stinging. When they take off and the stinger remains, it holds muscles, nerves, and parts of the digestive system with it. This barbed stinger is another way that worker bees are different from the queen. The queen does not have a barbed stinger. She has a smooth stinger, which is only used to kill any other competing females.

There is a lot of work to do in summer, and worker bees only live for about six weeks during that time. But in autumn, when there is hardly any work, the worker bees can live up to sixteen weeks. The type of work that they do is decided on the basis of their age. Younger bees, those that are three days old or younger, clean the cells. The ones who are three to six days old are responsible for feeding older larvae. Those who are six to ten days old feed the youngest larvae. Those who are eight to sixteen days old take pollen collected by the field bees. Bees who are between the ages of twelve and eighteen days make beeswax and build cells. Any bee that is older than fourteen days gather nectar, pollen, water, and rob weaker hives. Bees of this age can be guards, as well.

Drones

While the fertile eggs become female worker bees, infertile eggs develop into drones. Drones are male bees that exist solely to fertilize the queen. They have the longest period of development—twenty five days. During their developmental stages, not only do they need more time, they also require a larger cell than worker bees. Since summer is usually the swarm season, the production of drones starts in spring in most colonies so that they can reach peak population in summer. The life of a drone bee is around ninety days.

Drones do not head out of the hive to do field work, and they do not work inside the hive either. For this reason, they are usually driven out of the hives by worker bees in cold climates and left to die.

Even though the drones chiefly serve one purpose, they can perform other tasks. They can sense when the temperature in their hive is unsuitable. When that happens, they work with the worker bees to bring the temperature back to optimum. They either displace warm air with their wings or generate heat by shivering.

The Individual Bee

Bees are normally considered as a part of the collective, as they should be. (It is all their wings moving together that make their characteristic buzzing sound.) However, a single bee on his own, while he could not survive or do what he is meant to do, is a fascinating paradigm of evolution. Form has followed function beautifully in the anatomy and physiology of the honey bee.

A bee's purpose is to leave the hive to collect pollen. The bee's wings can create static electricity as it flies through the air and from plant to plant. This energy is used to attract the pollen particles, which then get stuck in the hair that covers its body. The bee's antennae can work as a thermometer, taking a temperature. They can also function in a way similar to the human nose. They can even measure oxygen and carbon dioxide levels.

Structure of hives

Information about the three main classes of bees is valuable, but that is not enough to be a good beekeeper. To achieve that, you must also know about their habitat. Bees plan their hives meticulously, and the knowledge of how they do that can be a considerable asset in your maintenance of the hives. It will also help you in the collection of produce.

Bees can reside in any space that will support their hive. An average bee hive is rectangular in shape. There are parallel frames inside the rectangular body, and they are used to house the eggs, larvae, and pupae. Food is also stored in them. If you were to cut along the frontal plane and examine the cross section of a bee hive, you would notice an ovoid, egg like, shape. Within this "egg", there are many hexagon-shaped cells that make up the honey honey comb. There are two honey combs on each side reserved for the storage of pollen and honey only. The brood nest in the center has a single frame housing the eggs, larvae and brood cells. These extend to the edge of the frame. Above the brood cells are cells filled with pollen. Above the pollen cells, there are cells filed with honey. It is these cells that form the top layer of the frame. Many of the honey combs hold honey, and extra honey is also stored in the honey combs above the brood. Honey has high energy content and pollen has high protein content. Both serve as food for the larvae.

Beekeepers have artificial hives, with boxes for different purposes. There is a "super" box above the brood box that allows you to take out the extra honey without harming the brood. A honey super is part of the beehive you will build that collects honey. It is a box that holds eight, nine, or ten hanging frames in which the bees can build and maintain their honeycombs. You should remember, however, to avoid taking out all the surplus honey present there. It is there to help the bees get through winter. If you do decide to remove all the honey, make sure to supplement what your bees have to feed on by giving them sugar water or corn syrup in autumn and winter.

Annual cycle of the bees

Every bee colony has an annual cycle. This annual cycle begins in spring and ends in winter. The brood nest expands rapidly with the onset of spring, which coincides with the availability of lots of pollen that is needed to feed to the larvae. The breeding continues from January throughout April and reaches its peak in May. By this time, a large number of bees are ready to collect nectar in the area.

All species do not hit the peak at the same time. This is due to the difference in rates of development from one species to another. Some of these differences have developed because of conditions in the region where the bees live. When the flowers in a particular region are in full bloom, the bees go out for harvesting. This period of time when the vegetation is in full bloom is known as the "nectar flow." After some time, the bees in the area began to develop and breed in such a way that their maximum population becomes active around the same time. Most regions only have a single nectar flow in a year, but some regions have two nectar flows every year. This also affects the development of bee population in that area.

Beekeepers must be able to predict the timing of the nectar flow. Being prepared for it ensures that you have a maximum active population of bees at that time. This does not come easy to most people, and you will miss the mark a few times before you get it right. You will also have to ensure your bees do not swarm. If they do and you cannot prevent it, you will have lost them even before the harvest season even starts. You will only get a minimum yield.

It is important to recognize the signs of an impending swarm. The first is the presence of larvae or egg cells in the queen's cells. Regular inspection will allow you to notice signs like this and begin preventative methods. Another sign is the appearance of queen cells or cells at the edge of the hive.

Methods for Preventing a Swarm

Preventing a swarm can be done in several ways. It is important to have more than one method in your skillset in the event that the first method that you try is ineffective.

Clipping and Marking Queens

One method of swarm prevention is called "queen clipping". While a queen bee has some unique physical characteristics, they can be difficult to pick out quickly, especially in larger colonies. Trapping and marking the queen is an important step in keeping track of her, her health, her activity, and her location.

If signs seem to point to a swarm, clipping the queen's wings can ensure that she stays in the hive. This involves amputating roughly a third of her wings, and must be done with great care so that no other body parts are involved.

Cutting Out Queen Cells

This method should not be relied on solely on its own, it must be applied in combination with other methods. It can be effective in honey combination with other methods, but requires absolutely diligent inspection. If even a single queen cell or swarm cell is missed at the edge of a hive, a swarm could begin without your knowledge.

Thomas Thatcher

Artificial Swarming

This process is intended to fool the bees into believing that they have already swarmed. It involves creating a second hive near the original and moving some pieces of the hive and some of the bees over to it.

One of the two will keep the old queen and a lot of bees, but only a small brood. It also maintains a collection of nectar and honey. The other will not have a laying queen, diverse ages of bees, and queen cells.

The Demaree Method

This method can be used to prevent swarming, replacing the queen, or for producing nuclei. It is unique because it involves transplanting the queen to a new brood box without queen cells and placing some extra queen excluders.

Congestion

A crowded hive is a hive prone to swarms. The best way to prevent a swarm, therefore, is to give the bees room and anticipate their needs for more room as their numbers swell.

Skilled beekeepers are able to prevent swarming, but also use swarming to their own advantage in the event that it does occur. They manage to contain the swarm within their own bee yard and allow them to form a hive there. The new swarm will produce more bees while the old one will create a new queen. Both the hives will continue to develop and increase their population. This can potentially double their harvest. The swarming should also take place in accordance with the nectar flow time of the area, so it is not as easy as it sounds. It takes experience to handle an impromptu swarming.

Chapter 2

Advantages of Beekeeping

This chapter is for those of you who are still hesitant about getting into beekeeping. If you are wondering why you should start beekeeping, read on.

Beekeeping Improves Crop Yields

Bees are adept at pollination. Unlike other insects, bees do not move from one species of plant to another. They stick to one plant and harvest pollen from only that, thus allowing good yield of plants. The bees will improve the health of your garden. In fact, bees are so effective that some farmers even pay beekeepers to cultivate bee hives in their farms so they can get better crop yields.

The Importance of Pollination

Pollination depends largely on insects like bees. We, in turn, depend enormously on pollination for our diets. One third of the food we eat is available to us because of bees pollinating plants and helping them to grow.

You Get Your Own Stock of Honey and Other Products

One hive can give you enough honey to use for an entire year. You will even have extra which you can sell in the market. Honey tastes delicious and is used widely in desserts, but it also has health benefits. The initial cost plus those costs you incur in maintaining the hive are not negligible, but the honey you get is still cheaper than buying it from the market, and you will also have honey to sell for potential profits.

You also get beeswax and other products from bees. This beeswax can be used to make candles, soaps, balms, and various other products. Beeswax is also used to polish wood. You will be saving money and getting pure beeswax which you can use or sell in the market.

Therapeutic Uses

Bee pollen is known to have therapeutic properties. Because of its high protein content, it is often used to treat allergies. When the pollen comes from the area around you, it can be the cause of allergies, but also a useful treatment.

Bees also produce propolis to keep their hives clean and fix gaps. Propolis is a resin, a semi-solid substance. It can be harvested from many plants, and has a variety of uses. The propolis found in a bee hive can be used as a pain remedy or as an antibacterial.

Even royal jelly has medical use because of its high vitamin B content. It is used to treat a variety of diseases, conditions, and complaints. Some of these common ailments that can be alleviated by the jelly are asthma, hay fever, insomnia, PMS, menopausal symptoms, skin disorders, and high cholesterol.

Honey has its own medicinal properties and has even been used by ancient people. It is a natural anti-inflammatory and can help with some wound care, allergy alleviation, coughs. Honey can even shrink and take the redness out of acne.

There is a whole branch of therapy that uses bee products to treat health problems. It is called apitherapy. They even use the venom from a bee sting, which you may think to be only harmful, to treat diseases. It has been shown to help in the successful treatment of arthritis.

Beekeeping and the Mind

Beekeeping also has a soothing effect on your mind, as believed by many practicing beekeepers. It is believed to be a stress reliever for many reasons. One is because it allows you to be one with nature, and spend time outside in the sun and air, which is important to mental health. The work it provides can keep a person's mind and body busy, which is healthy and can alleviate anxiety or depression. The humming of bees can also be very calming to a person because drone-like sounds are good at relieving stress and giving a feeling of calm.

While working closely with bees, it is important to keep a certain level of calm in the way you move and in your voice. Being quiet and moving slowing and deliberately are critical for the well-being of the bees. This behavior also has an interesting side effect. When we feel happy, we smile. When we feel calm, we move and speak in a certain way. This is not a one way street, however. By smiling, we can feel happier. By moving and speaking in a certain way, we can make ourselves feel calmer. The time spent with bees can give you an excuse and an opportunity to find almost meditative peace each day. This has been proven to have positive effects on blood pressure, immune system, and even concentration.

It is an educational hobby.

Bees are absolutely fascinating and working with them closely will help you understand many things about their behavior and nature. It is a good learning experience for everyone.

As you build your hive and come to manage the health and life of your bees, you will naturally reach out to other beekeepers or search for reading material to help you expand your knowledge base. This will lead to you becoming a curious person who seeks to learn and improve your mind.

It is one of the most rewarding hobbies.

Beekeeping does not require much investment. You do not even need to spend much time on it or have a lot of land to practice it. All it takes is a small garden

Thomas Thatcher

and some time from your schedule, and the rewards are abundant. You get a better garden, relief from stress, unadulterated bee products, and even economic benefits if you do it right.

Beekeeping

Chapter 3

How to Start

Beekeeping is rewarding, but it is not easy. Bees are not goldfish and need much more care and attention. They cannot be left to themselves with the exception of daily feeding. It may be less work than taking care of a pet dog, but it is still a lot of work. Especially if this hobby is to become a business anytime soon, you need to be able to do this properly.

We learned some basic knowledge about bees and hives in the previous chapters. We also learned about the advantages of beekeeping. In this chapter, we will learn how to actually start beekeeping. But before that, you need to answer an important question.

Are you ready to be a beekeeper?

This is the very first question every person should ask themselves before they start beekeeping. You need to know whether you are ready for it or not. And not only that, your family and even your neighbors should also be open to the idea of living around bees.

Before you get started, you need to make sure nobody in your family is allergic to bees. Most people are aware of these allergies if they have them, but some are not. Finding out is easy, however. Just go to a doctor and get a simple allergy test conducted to know whether anybody is allergic. Honeybees are not known to be very aggressive because they die after stinging someone. But you still need to be sure so that you can avoid any complications later.

Another thing you need to make sure of is that you have enough space for your bee colony. There should be some extra space to be safe so that your bees do not escape in case of an impromptu swarming. They need adequate space to build another hive in your field.

You will invest both your time and money into beekeeping, so consider how much of both you have to commit to it and whether that will be enough. The good news is that there is a range of time and money that can yield success in beekeeping.

Source of bees

You can obtain bees from a variety of ways, but some are more popular than others. The most popular ways are effective, safe, and will provide you with a healthy hive. They include the following: taking advantage of a swarm, baiting bees, buying from a breeder, nucleus colonies, and splits. It is a good idea to learn about each one and decide which you would like to try to begin your hive.

Swarms

Sometimes bees leave their hive along with their queen in search of a new home. This is called a swarm, and you can use these swarms to start a colony of your own. Since you will be catching natural bees (also known as feral bees), you will have the added advantage of having healthier bees. You will also have better prospects of splitting the colony because the bees will be healthy and strong. Only healthy and strong bees consider splitting. If they are weak, they will always stick together. Bees who are not at optimal health cannot survive away from their familiar hive. Since you will catch the bees from your local area, you can also be sure they will be acclimatized to your locale. This is considered the best way to start a colony.

Baiting

This is a relatively new technique being practiced by beekeepers. They bait boxes with old honey comb or with pheromones. They set these us near hives and make traps to capture bees. The feral bees are tricked into swarming and are then captured in the traps. Baiting is also a very effective method of obtaining bees and has similar advantages as swarming.

Packages

If you want to take the easier route, you can also buy bees from a bee breeder. These come in packages and the package usually contains one queen bee. This queen bee has been artificially inseminated and comes with ten thousand other bees from various colonies. The queen sits in a cage in the center so that the other bees in the box get used to her scent. They are shipped in a box that contains a can or bowl of sugar syrup. For the duration of shipping, this acts as their food supply.

Finding bee breeders should not be a hard task. You can easily find some who are located near you or ship to your location. Most breeders do not take the risk of shipping long distances because the bees might not survive such a long time in a box. It is also a torture for the bees and no breeder wants to subject their bees to that.

Nucleus Colonies

Nucleus colonies can be a superb way to start your bee colony, depending on the kind of hive you use. It is a fully developed colony that comes in a box with five frames. You can then transfer them to eight or ten frame boxes. Since they already have the eggs, larvae, nectar and honey inside them, they develop much faster than your average packages or swarms. The bees do not have to start from scratch. They just need to expand on what they already have.

You can find a nucleus colony at any reputed bee breeder's farm. Do an Internet search to find the ones nearest to you and take your pick.

Splits

Many beekeepers that use the top bar hives or Warre hives use a method known as the split. This is a method for those beekeepers that already have a bee farm. As the name suggests, the beekeepers take some bars that include brood, honey, and bees from a full colony and add it to a new hive. They can choose to take the queen or leave her behind. Whichever hive is queenless can raise a new one as long as some eggs are available in that hive. Some beekeepers even buy a queen bee and then put her in the queenless hive, but this method is frowned upon by the community because of the methods used in raising and inseminating queen bees.

A beekeeper's year

Once you have found bees and set up your hive, it is important to gain an understanding of what a beekeeper does at different times of year.

If you expect your bee colony to thrive, you will have to invest some time into it and be patient. Regular inspection of the hives during summer and other warm times will be crucial. In the warmer regions, like southern US, bees have longer foraging season. The ones raised in north do not enjoy such a long season. Winters hardly see any activity so your responsibilities to the hive will be at a minimum during this time. The bees are dormant and will not surface or do very much. During the rest of the year, however, you will have to constantly manage their hives. Let's look at the year in detail.

Spring

Spring is an important season because it is the time the queen starts laying eggs. You will have to constantly inspect the hive to check the progress of this. Another thing you will need to check is the proper storage of honey. If something is amiss with how the bees are storing the honey, your harvest will not be successful. Your inspections should also include looking for signs of disease in your bees. If you notice that your bees do not have enough honey to last till the first harvest, keep corn starch syrup or sugar ready. It will act as supplementary nutrition for them.

You will also need to get some medicines for your bees to help prevent any diseases. Medicate your bees every fortnight and continue to do this until a few weeks before summer. You should stop during the summer to make sure the medication does not get mixed in the honey.

Summer

Summer is a busy time for bees. They will have a larger supply of honey since they produce it at a higher rate. Put some extra sets of frames in your colony just before summer to make sure the hive does not collapse from all the extra honey. As their numbers grow and remain high, the hive could become crowded. Bees do not operate in cramped spaces. They will need their space, and if they feel the hive is congested, they will swarm and find a new place to build a hive. You do not want that to happen, so monitor your hives closely and add honey supers when you see the existing frames are filled up. You can remove the honey supers and extract the product once all the frames are filled with honey and more than half the cells are covered in wax. The bees will start needing less space once the season starts turning to autumn.

Fall

Once the honey is harvested, it is your decision whether you want to keep the bees or not. If you want to buy a new package in the next spring season, you can get rid of your bees. Most people do not do that, however. They keep their bees throughout the winter and then use the same bees in the next summer. If you plan to do so, make sure you have everything prepared for the winter. Examine the hive for any diseases and medicate the colony appropriately. Make sure they have enough food to pass the winter. If they do not, you will have to feed them water and sugar. Most people feed them by September to make sure they have enough food supply till the winter ends. The total weight of the hive should also be above one hundred twenty five pounds. This includes the bottom, honey supers, lid, pollen, bees, and the honey. If your colony is not too big, move it indoors. If you cannot do that, wrap it to protect it from the harsh winter.

Winter

If you have decided to leave the bees outside with protection, you have done your job. There is not much else that you can do. Even when completely covered in snow, they can survive, so you need not worry. If you have kept them indoors, make sure the room temperate does not fluctuate. Keep it at about five degrees Celsius—it is what they are used to during this season. In addition to the temperature control, the bees have other needs. The room should be well ventilated too.

A beekeeper's starting kit

Like any other job or hobby, there are certain tools that help you do the work of beekeeping well. Higher quality products will last longer, but may be more of an investment than you are willing to make when you first start beekeeping. Shopping around, researching different brands of each piece of equipment, and even asking more experienced beekeepers about their own preferences will all help you to find the right tools for you and your needs and plans.

Hive tool

It is the absolute "must have" tool for any beekeeper. The hive tool helps you inspect the hives and add new boxes to them. It is used to detach the sides of a have. It can also scrape off excess wax. In a bee hive, everything is glued together with propolis as we have already discussed. The hive tool is used to break open the gum gently, and scrape off the propolis if necessary.

This tool looks is a flat piece of metal about ten inches long. It curves at one end like the letter J and flares at the other end.

Smoker

The smoker is what we use to subdue the bees. The smoke can mask their alarm pheromones so that the guards' response does not alert the rest of the colony and the bees allow the keeper to inspect the hive.

Honeybees are not aggressive creatures, so they will be calm most days. But sometimes, you will find that they are very agitated. It is better to avoid the hives on such days, but if you really need to inspect the hives, you will have to use the smoker.

This piece of equipment is available in many different sizes. It looks like a can with a funnel on top. On the side of it, it has what looks like a bellows that helps pump the smoke into the can and out of the spout.

Jacket with veil

Beginners are not very comfortable with the idea of their bare hands and face so close to the bees. They can get stung any time, and that prospect makes it harder for them to enjoy beekeeping. So as a beginner, it is better to buy yourself some protective gear and wear it until you become confident around bees. This includes a jacket, a veil and a pair of gloves at the very least. If you want to go all out, buy a full body suit. There is nothing better than that.

Beginners are usually nervous around bees, and bees can sense it. They are more likely to sting you if you are nervous or worried because you will make more mistakes in that state. You do not want to get stung in your early days, as it will only deter you from pursuing this hobby. So wear protection and stay comfortable around your bees. You can continue to use the veil for however long you want.

Bee brush

If you do not want the bees to be around a particular part of the honey comb, you can use the bee brush to gently brush them away. Be warned, however, because the bees do not like the brush. In fact, they absolutely hate it. So they will always try to sting the brush, and in that, you can lose a lot of bees. Use the bee brush sparingly.

One technique that has been useful and has, at least anecdotally, proven to be less distressing to the bees is this. By using only the top two inches of the brush with slow, light strokes, the bees are less disturbed. It should also be noted that the beekeeper describing this method also recommended moving the brush from the bottom up. This made the smoker unnecessary and stopped the bees from stinging.

Thomas Thatcher

When should I start a bee colony?

This is another important question that you need to ask yourself. There is no right answer for this question because the pattern followed by the bees greatly depends on the climate in your region. So the hive activity will vary depending on where you live. The best way for you find out a suitable time is by contacting other beekeepers and bee breeders in your area. Talk to them about the habits of bees in your area. Once you have learned about the most active months and when the bees in the area are generally mating and hatching, you will be better prepared for your future bees' cycles throughout the year. You can then spend the winter planning how you will go about starting your bees and what each time of the year will require of you. Take note of all the details, they can provide you with the knowledge needed to be prepared for whatever the year throws at you.

There are other ways to meet and pick the brains of more experienced beekeepers. You can also join a local beekeeping club or organization to help you learn more about bees and current trends in apiculture. You can socialize and share tips with other beekeepers. Trust me, beekeepers love to talk bees.

Beekeeping

Chapter 4

Taking It to the Next Level

Now that you have got the hang of the basics, it is time to step into some advanced territory. We have learned about bees, their annual cycle, the required equipment, and other basic things. In this chapter, we will study some more advanced concepts and learn about equipment that will help you take your hobby to the next level.

Hives

An average hive will have a bottom board and a cover. It has at least five honey supers in between the bottom and the cover, each of them containing ten frames of honey combs. The honey and pollen are stored in these honey combs, and they also provide rearing grounds for young bees. The young ones are reared in the lowermost honey supers while the others are used for storage.

You can build your own hive and then introduce bees to it, but it is not a great method since bees do not like new environments. They might get stressed and not produce enough honey, and you cannot afford that. So it is better if you just purchase a package with a hive.

Make sure the hive you use, whether built or bought, is of a standard size. The brood cells should be able to house the worker bees well enough. They should not be too small. Also, remember to keep your bees disease free by medicating them regularly. If you decide to buy the bees with the hives, do it during spring season.

Which beehive is the best?

The beehive that is best for you is not necessarily the largest or most expensive. This completely depends on what you expect from beekeeping. What I mean to say is that if you want to get a lot of honey so that you can sell it, you will go for a different hive. But if you only need enough to use at home and maybe give to family and friends, you might want to go for a different type of hive. Most commonly, beekeepers use the Top Bar Hive, the Langstroth Hive, and the Warre Hive. They all have their own advantages and disadvantages. As with the equipment, research into the respective merits of each type would be a good use of your time. Talking to beekeepers about which hives they like, why they use the one they do, and how much honey they yield can be an even better way to learn about each type of hive before you buy. This is prudent before such a large investment.

Top Bar Hive

The top bar hive is one of the oldest types of hives in use. Also known as the horizontal top bar hive, it is a long cavity which has a lot of wooden bars laid across on top of it. The bees start building their honey combs from the lowest point and fill up the cavity as they go up adding more honey combs. By the time it is finished, it looks like slices of bread lying next to each other.

The great thing about this model is that it allows you to keep increasing the number of bars as the bees keep filling them up with honey combs and require more room. If you add a false back, you can continue to expand the hive as much as you want. If you do this in a systematic way, the bees will also build their honey combs in an ordered manner. Top bar hives happen to be the cheapest hive model out of all. You can use cheap materials to build them and there is no need to use expensive tools and such. They were first introduced in Africa as an alternative to other expensive models.

Since top bar hives do not have stacking frames, they are pretty lightweight. Extracting honey from them is easy and you do not need an extractor for it. You can just harvest it directly if you feel like the hive is getting a bit too full. You will have to cut the honey combs from the bars, so you can either crush them to collect the honey or sell them as they are. You can also collect clear honey and separate it from the wax if you strain it. You can then use the wax to make candles or balms.

Langstroth Hive

In North America, this one is the most preferred hive model. Invented by Reverend Lorenzo Langstroth in the nineteenth century, its defining feature is the movable frame.

The Langstroth hive uses three types of boxes – shallow, medium and deep – stacked upon each other. The shallow boxes are the shortest and the deep boxes are the tallest. As a beginner, it is best if you start with two deep or three medium boxes. They all come in widths of eight frames and ten frames. If you want your hives to be lightweight, you should go with the eight frame boxes. They also allow all parts to be interchangeable. Most people still prefer to use the ten frame boxes, however.

You can keep adding more boxes on the top as your bee colony expands. This process is known as supering, the extra boxes being known as honey supers. Once your honey supers are filled, you can remove them and harvest the surplus supply for your own use or to sell.

There is a foundation inside each frame. It is comprised of nothing but a thin sheet made of plastic or beeswax. These sheets are pressed into hexagonal patterns, which mimics the natural shape of the honey comb and will promote building. The bees draw out the foundation when they are added to the hive, and they create cells to store honey and develop the brood. The foundation can also have wires running through it to reinforce it and make it stronger. This system also makes it easy to harvest. When you need to take out the honey, you can simply remove the foundation and frames, and then cut off the caps from the cells. The caps are made of wax and serve as a protection for the vulnerable honey comb and the precious store of honey it holds. Removing the wax caps is not too difficult, and once it is gone you will be able to harvest. This can be done through the use of an extractor and you will be able to easily collect the honey.

Warre Hive

The Warre Hive is the invention of a French monk by the name of Emile Warre. He developed it in the twentieth century as a sensible and cost-effective way to build a hive. Before he settled on this model, he prototyped and experimented with over two hundred fifty hives. Warre would come to call it the "people's hive".

In this model, there is a stack of boxes with eight top bars, similar to the horizontal top bar. These bars are evenly spaced above each box in the stack and the bees proceed to build their honey combs from each bar. As compared to the Langstroth hive, the boxes are much smaller. This is because Warre wanted to provide the bees with cells as close to their natural cells as possible, and he found that the cells bees lived in naturally were much smaller than what the other hive models had.

Unlike the Langstroth hive, in the Warre hive, the boxes are not added to the top of the hive. Instead, they are added to the bottom of the hive. This might seem illogical to some of you, but if you look at how bees operate in nature, you will see that they build their honey combs from the top to the bottom. So it is much more natural for the bees to have extra building space on the bottom than on the top, as that is how they build in nature. In the Langstroth hive model, the bees are forced to build their honey combs from the bottom to the top. They see this odd structure as an obstacle they must overcome, and so they adjust to the circumstances. In actuality, Bees can build in any direction, and in any shape. If they have space on the right, they will build more honey combs on the right. This is also true for the space being to the left or above their heads, as discussed with the Langstroth hive. However, the most natural thing for them to do is to build downwards, and that is exactly what they are able to do in the Warre hive.

As you keep adding boxes at the bottom, the bees keep moving their brood nest downwards. The honey stores stay on the top boxes, and it forms an easy and natural way to remove honey combs. It helps you maintain a healthy and repeatable cycle of honey comb removal, which is essential for the health and continued existence of any colony. So in this method, you can keep adding boxes to the bottom and removing the ones on the top to take out the surplus.

Thomas Thatcher

Where should I put my hive?

Before you begin setting up, there is a lot to consider. One of the first things to make a decision about is the location of your hive. For you to decide the best place to put your hive, you need to consider several factors. These include your access to it, its access to sun and water, the topography, the safety concerns of your neighbors and neighborhood, and the flora of the area where you live.

Ease of access

This is the most important factor when it comes to deciding the placement of your hives. You should be able to access it easily. Bees can overcome any obstacle you throw their way and have few physical limitations, but it is not true for humans. If you are unable to access the hives easily, that could be a big problem. So make sure your hive is placed at a location that allows you to stand or kneel comfortably. It is even better if you place them in a roomier location where there is space for at least two people to fit in.

Early morning sun

It is important for hives, especially the ones in colder areas, to receive good sunlight. When hives are lit by the early morning sun, they are more productive because it helps bees maintain their natural cycle. It does not make much difference in hot areas, but early morning is very essential for bee hives in chilly areas.

By considering where the sun hits in your yard at certain times of day, you can plan for the best location to set up the hive for the bees' health.

Water source

Another important thing for bees is access to water. You should never use your neighbor's pool as a water source for your bees. It is better to build a shallow pool or a bird path in your own yard. It is essential for the bees, so make sure you provide them a water source.

Dehydration is very serious for bees, as it is for most living creatures. Without quick access to water, they may leave the area in search of it, which would be detrimental to the population in your hive. They could also die without sufficient water to maintain life.

Flat area

Bees are sensitive to the orientation of their hive, so if their hive is slanted, they will build honey combs that way. It is preferable to avoid slanted honey combs, as it will only create trouble for you while removing them. So place your hives on a flat surface and make sure it is parallel to the ground.

Presence of forage

Bees need to collect pollen and nectar, so it is important that they have sufficient flowering plants in the nearby area. You cannot control the amount of flora in your area, but you sure can plant a lot of flowering plants in your own backyard and immediate vicinity. If you have a park nearby, that is even better.

By providing your bees with a varied and plentiful selection of plant life, you are allowing them to live as naturally as possible. Diverse plant life in the area around the hive also provides the bees with the opportunity to collect pollen from different flora.

Safety

Safety is a very important factor when you are starting beekeeping. It is not only about the safety of your bees but also the safety of your family and neighbors. Make sure you build high fences around your property if your neighbors are not comfortable with having bees around their houses. This will deter the bees from going out of your property. You should also protect your bee hive by placing it in a place where natural elements cannot hurt it.

Legal issues

You should be aware of all the laws regarding beekeeping in your area. If it is not legally acceptable to raise bees in your city, you will not be able to take it on as a hobby or as a way to make a living. However, with proper paperwork and permissions, most cities allow beekeeping. Some places make it very difficult to get a beekeeping license, and some others ban the usage of certain models of hives. You should stay up-to-date on all the laws and regulations governing beekeeping in your area.

Extraction equipment

Depending on the type of hive you use, you will most likely require certain tools to harvest honey from your bee hives. The first step in the process is to separate the honey combs without damaging them or killing the bees. For a small operation with only a few bees, a bee brush is fine for moving bees away from where you need to work. You can gently sweep the bees away and then proceed to separate the honey combs. However, in a large-scale farm, it is very tedious to use a bee brush, and there is an added risk of losing a lot of bees in the process. An alternative in that situation is the use of escape boards. With the help of escape boards, you can direct the bees in particular directions and get them to move away from the area where you need to collect or remove honey combs.

You can also use chemicals such as Bee Go or Bee Robber. The smell of these chemicals makes the bees fly away from the area, thereby leaving the honey combs free for harvesting. But these chemicals require their own special covers called acid boards. If you follow the manufacturer's instructions, the odor will not remain and affect the honey.

Another option to separate honey combs is the bee blower. You can place a stand right outside the hive and then use the blower to blow the bees out. The disadvantage with the bee blower is that it is cumbersome, looking similar to a snow or leaf blower. It is also expensive. It is not the best option for someone starting out with beekeeping. For those who are more established and ready to make such an investment, or for somebody who has a large colony, a bee blower will work well and be worth the purchase.

Once you have separated the honey combs, you can extract the honey. Hand powered extractors can handle two frames at a time while motor powered ones can handle even one hundred or more simultaneously. Extractors are expensive, however, so you may want to start out by buying used extractors instead of new ones. If you feel like expanding your operation, you can buy new ones later and even invest in a big extractor.

Another thing you will need is an electrically heated knife. This will help you remove wax cappings from the honey combs. This wax lays over the honey comb, protecting the honey.

For a small hobby operation, a nylon or cheesecloth can be used to strain the honey. You will need two buckets, one with the honeycomb inside and the other with the cheesecloth covering the top of the bucket. The honey will be placed on top of the cheesecloth and the wax will be left over on the cloth. You will want to cut the honeycomb up inside the bucket, into small pieces to release the honey. Then take large handfuls (make sure your hands are thoroughly clean) and place on the cheesecloth for straining. You can leave the cheesecloth and honeycomb along until all the honey is drained out of the comb. When the honey is almost all drained into the bucket, you can squeeze the remaining remnants of the honeycomb to release the last of the honey. Depending on the type of plant or tree used, honey will be different colors.

After that, you have to store it in a warm place, allowing the impurities to rise to the top. For those who want to turn this into a proper business, it makes sense to invest into a tank with an outlet at the bottom to help collect filtered honey.

Equipment for the winter

As we have already discussed, it is important for you to protect your hives from the cold. For that, you will need insulation to wrap around your hives. Make sure the hive is fully and properly covered, and then cover it with plastic to keep the insulation in place. You can then cover the hives in wooden boxes and tie it to something sturdy to prevent wind damage. Winter is a dormant time.

Chapter 5

Diseases and Treatments

Varroa mites

Varroa jacobsoni and Varroa destructor are two species of parasitic mites that commonly attack bees. They survive on the bodily fluids secreted by the bees. If you see brown or red spots on the thorax of your bees, then they have been infected by these mites. These mites also act as carriers for viruses which make them even more dangerous to the bees. They are particularly lethal when the hive is already weakened by a preceding disease or weather condition. If the hive is weak enough, they can destroy it in a single attack. These mites tend to attack drones more than worker bees or the queen bee. Once bees realize that there are mites close by, they leave the hive in a swarm.

There are a number of treatments that you can employ to get rid of these mites. The treatments are usually classified into mechanical and chemical treatments. The mechanical treatments include the disruption of the lifecycle of the mite. Such methods do not necessarily lead to the eradication of these mites. They are usually used to keep the mite's population under control. Some examples of mechanical methods are brood interruption, powdered sugar dusting, and drone brood sacrifice. Unlike mechanical methods, chemical methods aim to completely destroy the mite population. There are two types of chemical treatments commonly used. Once is the hard chemical treatment which includes Amitraz (Apivar is the market name) and Coumaphos (Market name is CheckMite). The other type is the soft chemical. These include oxalic acid, thymol (Market names include Apiguard and ApiLife-Var) and formic acid. Before you use these chemicals make sure that you check the regulations in your area for these chemicals. Also, make sure that you do not sell the honey produced during the time you treat the hives with chemicals since the honey might contain high amounts of these chemicals.

Small hive beetles

Aethina tumida are small beetles that are found in hives. These beetles originated in Africa and made their way into North America. The pupae live buried in the ground surrounding hives. Once the pupae mature and develop, they migrate into the hives. Beekeepers often use ant eradication chemicals to keep these beetles out of the hives. Diatomaceous earth is one other possibility that can be tried. The diatoms in diatomaceous earth get stuck onto the beetles' skin. This causes them dehydrate and eventually die. Several pesticides are also commonly used to get rid of these beetles. Honey combat Roach Gel is the market name of Fipronil, which is commonly used to drive away these beetles by applying it to the corrugations. Corrugations trap the beetles but do not the bees. Hence, the bees do not come in contact with the pesticide. Hence, it is one of the safest chemical methods to get rid of beetles.

Nosema

Another organism that can make honey bees quite ill and threaten the colony is *Nosema apis*. Also known as nosemosis, this parasite invades the intestinal tracts of adult bees. It becomes a particular problem in winter or other times when the bees are unable to leave the hive and eliminate waste away from where they are living.

There are multiple ways to treat and prevent nosema disease. It can be treated by increased ventilation and antibiotics. It can be prevented by careful management, especially by removing as much honey as possible before winter begins. In the interim, you can feed the bees on sugar water. While some in the apicultural community will criticize this practice because of the nutritional properties of refined sugar, it can prevent this dangerous disease.

One potential risk factor for nosemosis is exposure to corn pollen containing certain genes. Research could not confirm this, but seemed to suggest that it is slightly more likely that bees will develop *Nosema apis* after exposure.

Wax Moths

These moths do not attack the honey bees but eat the wax that protects the honey comb. They need a protein in used brood honey comb to develop fully. The destroyed honey comb can lead to contamination of honey and even kill larvae.

The good news for beekeepers living in colder climates, like North America, is that wax moths cannot survive in cold weather. Additionally, bees can take care of wax moths themselves and will kill and control the population.

Cripaviradae-Chronic Bee Paralysis Virus

This virus has two forms, only named "Syndrome 1" and "Syndrome 2".

The first, Syndrome 1, includes tremors in the wings and body. The wings are spread, dislocated, and do not allow flight. The honey sac of these bees is distended, which gives them a bloated abdomen. They can crawl up plant stems, and often huddle together.

Bees suffering from the second form, Syndrome 2, can fly initially, but are hairless. Their appearance changes as they become dark and smaller. Their abdomen becomes broader. The other bees in the colony turned on the affected, attacking them and even trying to stop them at the entrance to the hive. Before long, the tremors begin as in Syndrome 1. After this, they lose the ability to fly and perish.

Dicistroviridae

There are some viruses related to cripaviradae, known as dicistroviridae. They include the following: acute bee paralysis virus, Israeli acute paralysis virus, Kashmir bee virus, and black queen virus.

Many of this type of virus are related to colony collapse disorder.

Colony Collapse Disorder

Colony collapse disorder happens when a colony is left without most of the worker bees. The queen remains, as do nurse bees to take care of the larval bees. There is usually enough honey, but this leads to the loss of a hive.

The frequency of this phenomenon has increased greatly in recent years, the causes for which are hotly debated. Some possible causes include mite infections, genetics, malnutrition, lack of immunity, and one type of pesticide.

Some signs that you might see in your hive will include unhatched but abandoned brood, food stores that are generally left alone, a young workforce, a smaller than normal workforce, and bees' reluctance to take in supplementary nutrition. You will not find dead bees or any of the common mites that can kill or harm bees. The bees have disappeared.

There are some ways that the Mid-Atlantic Apiculture Research and Extension Consortium recommend to manage this disorder. One of these is to keep strong colonies away from weaker ones. Another is to replace sugar syrup or other supplements to their food with Fumagilin.

This is a relatively new condition to be discovered and named. An experienced, professional beekeeper brought it to the world's attention in 200. Since then, scientists have worked tirelessly to solve this mystery.

Colony collapse disorder has been documented in thirty five states. In each of these states, beekeepers and scientists took samples of the pollen, wax, honey, combs, and whatever bees they could find. The bees that they were able to perform autopsies on revealed several pathogens and other problems. This led to the theory that there is an immune system issue developing among honey bees. The bodies of bees are in short supply, however, because, as previously discussed, colony collapse disorder does not leave behind a lot of dead bees. Instead, they have disappeared. They could be abandoning their hives, sensing the likelihood of becoming infected and being unable to fight it.

This is perhaps the direst problem faced by both honey bees and beekeepers. It is a manifestation of one of the most serious threats to our species' well-being and survival.

While many beekeepers have found that splitting a hive can fill any gaps created by colony collapse disorder, the United States of America has still needed to import bees from other countries in order to keep up with the pollination demands that we have.

Foulbrood

There are two common types of foulbrood that affect bees. One of them is the European foulbrood. The causative organism of European foulbrood is the bacteria, *Melissococcus plutonius*. This infects the midgut of bee larvae. The bacterial cells can survive for at least a few months on just beeswax. Symptoms of this particular disease type are brown or yellow colored larvae that are usually dead. This disease is often considered as a stress disease because it is usually lethal only when the hive is already under some kind of stress. The other type of foulbrood is the American foulbrood. This is much more deadly and infectious when compared to the European foulbrood. It is the most destructive bee disease. It is caused by *Paenibacillus larvae.* It can affect larvae that are as young as twenty four hours. The spores of this microorganism grow in the gut by draining all the nutrients from the larvae. Hence, the larvae invariably die in their sealed cells because the microorganism is taking away all the nutrients. The bacteria die once the larvae die because its food source is dead. However, before it dies it produces millions of spores that are extremely durable. These spores can survive for decades till they find the right conditions to grow and develop. They are sometimes even found on beekeeping equipment. Even though it only infects larvae, it can cause the death of an entire colony just by killing all the larvae.

Ocytetracycline is a chemical that is often used to kill these bacteria. However, you have to remember not to use the honey produced during the treatment period because it will contain varying levels of chemical residue that could be harmful to us. Shook Swarm is another method that is being considered as a replacement for the chemical method. Prophylactic methods of treatment should be avoided since they could lead to the bacteria becoming resistant to the treatment.

Stonebrood

Aspergillus fumigates, Aspergillus flavus and *Aspergillus Niger* are the three fungi that cause the disease known as Stonebrood. This disease causes a change in composition of the brood that makes them appear mummified. Each of these three fungi has spores that are different in shape. These fungi can also affect animals and humans leading to a number of respiratory disorders. When these spores attack the larvae, they manage to enter the bee larvae. They tend travel to the gut where they hatch and grow rapidly. This leads to the formation of a ring like band near the head of the larvae. Once the larvae die, they turn black and become hard, making it difficult to crush them; hence the name Stonebrood. The spores then take over the body of the dead larvae and form a layer over it. If the worker bees manage to clean out the dead larvae then there is a possibility that the hive will not become completely infected by the fungi. Otherwise, it may completely wipe out the entire bee population in the hive.

Iflaviridae or deformed wing virus

This disease, caused by a virus *Iflaviridae*, is known to cause wing deformities amongst other deformities. It is usually transmitted into the bee through the parasitic mite, *Varroa destructor*. The deformities are taken in when the parasite infects the pupae in a hive. If the parasite happens to infect an adult bee, they rarely develop any symptoms of the disease. On some occasions, they might show a change in behavior. Deformed bees are usually those that are infected when they were in the pupae stage. Deformed bees are normally chased out of the hive and left to die. If the number of deformed bees in a hive is large, then there is a chance for the colony to die out.

These are just some of the common diseases that infect bees. In order for you to take precautions against these diseases, as well as others, it would better if you read up on various bee diseases before embarking on beekeeping. Besides the diseases caused by various other micro or macro organisms, bees are also highly susceptible to pesticides. Hence, make sure that you do not raise your bees anywhere near areas that are filled with pesticides. Just make sure that they do not get exposed to any sort of pesticides or other stray chemicals used by your neighbors or in the vicinity of your land.

Chapter 6

Additional Income: Starting A Small Beekeeping Operation

Why Beekeeping as a Business?

Once a person begins beekeeping, they realize that their "hobby" has the potential to turn into an area of additional income. The excess production of wax and honey from your current personal operation is suddenly overwhelming your home, filling extra cupboards, closets, and pantries. There's only so much honey and wax you can give as presents! Once you experience this, maybe it is time to start making additional income from what you though was "just a hobby".

Last year, North Dakota, the leader in honey production, produced 33,120,000 pounds of honey, resulting in $67,565,000 in sales. The total consumption of honey in the United States is approximately 410 million pounds a year. The average individual consumes 1.3 pounds of honey a year according to the National Honey Board. Half of all honey sold is through retail stores, the other half is sold in bulk to manufacturers or wholesalers.

The agriculture industry and many crops, in general, are dependent on honey bee pollination. In 2010, according to a Cornell University study, beekeeping pollination contributed to $19 billion dollars in additional agricultural crops. Farmers and companies that depend on agricultural products are completely dependent on the honey bee in order to continue to make an income and produce food for the American people. In addition, the beeswax that is also produced from honey bees helps pollinated agricultural crops, gardens, and habitats for wildlife. It is estimated that 80% of crop pollination is accomplished by honey bees, resulting in one-third of the American diet originates either directly or indirectly, from pollinated agricultural products.

On of the biggest agricultural industries in the United States is the production of almonds. The biggest producer of almonds is California, producing 82% of the world's almonds, 70% of that production is exported internationally. In 2013, the number one U.S. export was almonds, 20 times more than wine, the second largest exported good. Almonds not only contribute to income for Californians but contribute to the national economy due to interstate commerce. It cannot be said almonds are unimportant; almonds continue to provide jobs for American people, feed people national and in other countries, and support the national as well as international economy. Thus, it is very important to highlight that without honey bees almonds would not exist!

Almond crops are completely dependent on honey bee pollination. California currently has 790,000 acres of almond crops, these farmers need over a million colonies of honey bees to sustain this kind of production and number of acres that California farmers use for production. Other crops, such as apples, avocados, blueberries, sunflowers, cherries, and cranberries are 90% dependent on honey bee pollination as well.

In addition, the food used to feed another is one of the largest industries in the United States. For example, the meat production industry is made from crops that are completely dependent on honey bee pollination as well. The meat industry is the largest division of United States agriculture. In many states where the largest amount of meat is produced, the economy is dependent on meat production to sustain their economy. As you can see, the bee industry is very important to many industries that produce the world's food.

The importance of bees doesn't stop there, however, beauty products use beeswax to make creams, lotions, lip balm, and many other self care products. There is recent concern about using products that contain petroleum oil and mineral oil, stating these oils are derived from crude oil and have adverse health effects.

Thus, the use of beeswax is far preferred for use in beauty products.

Beeswax is also used for natural soap and candle production. Candles account for $2 billion of the nation's economy; seven out of ten households have candles in their home. They are used for holidays, special celebrations, and decoration. It goes without saying the importance of soap as well, I'm sure you have come across natural soap in a retail store once or twice. So now you're starting to get an idea of the many uses of beeswax and the industries it supports!

Getting Started

Beekeepers have steadily declined over the last 50-60 years due to land development that made beekeeping difficult to sustain. However, the decline in beekeeping and beekeepers have shown the world just how important the practice is. Now the number of people starting beekeeping is back on the rise and that's a good thing. People are more aware of the amazing uses for honey and beeswax, as well as the economies that depend on honey bees. Knowing this, it is easy to see why you want to start your own beekeeping operation to generate extra income, but you'd probably be surprised to know that start-up costs are relatively reasonable and inexpensive.

An individual can manage up to 500-1,000 colonies on their own, however, anything over this and the task can be overwhelming and physically impossible. Many people will choose not to have anywhere near this number of colonies on their own, but it is good to know what the maximum is before you start your business.

An alternative way to start beekeeping is to search for an experienced beekeeper that currently oversees a commercial operation. If you show enough enthusiasm and hard work an experienced beekeeper may not only offer to teach you but show you the way through extra help. Eventually, you can work out a retirement plan when the beekeeper chooses to retire, you can be made in charge of the operation. This is a lot like apprenticeships hundreds of years ago. Learning through doing can be extremely helpful and many new beekeepers learn better this way.

Even if this is not the way you want to go initially, talking with experienced beekeepers and keeping in contact will definitely help. Joining a local beekeeping club or organization will help when situations arise that you are not familiar with, and being a part of the industry will keep you appraised of the latest news and information.

When the environment the bees are kept in is relatively calm, and plenty of food and water is supplied, the bees will thrive. Be aware that many bees can produce a swarm, which is great for your honey production, however, neighbors my not appreciate this. Bees also can find other places besides their colonies to live, including holes in walls, basements, and attics. If one of these places happens to be your neighbor's, your beekeeping activity will probably not be tolerated by your neighbors.

As previously mentioned, you will want to check with local laws and ordinances to make sure that it is legal to set up hives or colonies in your region. You will also want to make sure beehives are allowed within city limits or within the borders of your hometown. Always be sure to be a responsible beekeeper, if nuisances related to the keeping of your bees emerge frequently, it is possible that anti-beekeeping legislation could be enacted. Make sure you are following all laws. This point is reemphasized in order to make sure your investment does not go to waste!

Also, be aware of the potential for the intrusion of the African honey bee as they are very aggressive. Typically, the best way to keep them from entering your area is to have an established managed hive. Although African honey bee stings are not more painful than regular honey bees, they can swarm, be more aggressive and cause more damage.

Harvesting Cycle

The harvesting season typically occurs in the spring. After harvesting, the bees survive off of stored honey and pollen until the season begins again. Some bees can survive up to six months on stored honey, but it is important to make sure plenty of food and water are available for the bees to survive. To protect the bees during the cold months, ensure all the hive components are weather tight and safe from the elements. Wind, rain, or snow can significantly harm your colony and deplete the honey for next year. During the cold seasons, bees tend to refrain from much activity, however, when the weather is warm, bees will continue to fly around. When this occurs, the bees increase their activity and tend to deplete their reserves faster. Make sure when you harvest the honey, you take into account the weather temperature and the activity level of your bees so enough reserves are left.

When temperatures are below 50 degrees F, bees head to their hive to get warm. As the temperatures continue to drop, honey bees will gather in a central area within the hives and create a "winter cluster". A winter cluster is much like a "huddle" or "scrum". The bees pack closely together to warm their bodies up and stay like this all winter.

The one job for the honey bees during the winter is to keep the queen bee alive and warm. This works by all the worker bees clustering around the queen bee and fluttering their wings or shivering to create warm and energy. The constant movement keeps the hive warm during the cold winter months.

In order for each bee to keep warm, bees on the outside of the cluster slowly rotate towards the center while the bees towards the center rotate towards the outside. The temperature of the cluster can range from 45 degrees F on the outside of the cluster, to 80 degrees F in the center of the cluster. The colder the weather outside, the tighter the bees cluster together to provide warmth.

In order for the worker bees to produce all this energy, there must be a source of food to provide sustenance. This comes in the form of stored honey. There must be enough honey to last the whole winter until bees can start collecting pollen again. Therefore, knowing how much pollen to take is very important.

The harvesting season is an annual occurrence; once the time comes, transferring the honey from the hives takes several steps as previously outlined. After the honey is extracted and spun, the honey is poured into glass jars for retail sales. Labels are placed on the jars with your brand name, right before going to sell.

Essential Equipment for the Small Beekeeper Operation

Although we discussed the type of equipment you need to get started and additional important equipment when you are ready to expand your knowledge, there is essential equipment you will need if you decide to start your own beekeeping operation. Depending on the size of your operation, you may need vehicles to move your equipment, bees, and storage. However, many small operations are limited in distance between each hive, so if you have 3-4 colonies, you probably only have to walk a maximum of 40-50 feet to monitor and harvest. Each colony is recommended to be between 6-10 feet apart.

In addition to the equipment described in previous chapters, you'll also need hives, fume boards, queen excluders, feeders, entrance reducers, robbing screens, follower boards, bee brush, veil and hat, smoker and hive tool, white coveralls, and elbow length gloves.

Don't forget the bees! You can purchase a "package" of bulk bees complete with a queen and start them out in an empty hive. You can also purchase a current operation colony, hives, and all the equipment, from an established beekeeper. A "nuc" or nucleus colony is a package with a queen, some worker bees, brood, and food. Nucs can be purchased with three to five frames to place in an empty hive. The last option, but also one of the riskiest, is to find your own swarm of bees and capture them for your hive. You can contact local law enforcement or fire department to inquire about nuisance swarms to relocate. Of course, law enforcement will be more than happy to have someone help take this job off their hands, but beware of the type of swarm you are relocating. Chances are if bees have swarmed before, they are more likely to do it again. Secondly, bees that have previously swarmed tend to be more aggressive and more difficult to integrate with other honey bees. They also may come with parasites or diseases to watch for. You can try to control the swarm and prevent it from occurring again by replacing the queen bee with a new queen bee that is less aggressive.

Costs

The costs to begin a small scale commercial operation (this is an operation greater than your backyard requiring 10-20 acres of land) are not unreasonable or expensive. You can start small, of course. Begin by approaching your local natural foods stores, health stores, and farmers markets to see the demand for your kind of product. Talk to local boutiques or natural skin care retailers and ask if you can place your product in their store to sell. Researching the market is very important prior to making an investment. You should also spend some time thinking about your product. What is more interesting for you to make? Honey or beeswax items? You could sell your honeycomb in bulk to wholesalers or you can sell your honey in bulk, and keep the beeswax for making your own product or sell to make-up lines or skin care manufacturers. There is a lot of potential and profitability from beekeeping as a profession.

The University of California provides the following information on cost and supplies to get started as a small scale commercial beekeeping operation. These costs are for the operation of 1,000 colonies and they can easily be divided down to fit your needs.

For the Production and Support of 1,000 Colonies

1,000 bottom boards at $8 each - $8,000

1,000 covers at $8 each - $8,000

2,000 deep boxes at $12 each - $24,000

20,000 deep frames at $0.35-$0.65 - $10,000

20,000 deep foundations at $0.06 - $1,200

1,000 medium depth boxes at $8 each - $8,000

10,000 medium depth fames at $0.40 each - $4,000

10,000 medium depth foundation at $0.40 - $4,000

100,000 frame eyelets at $2.00 per 1,000 - $200

2,000 queen excluders (optional) $9.00 each - $18,000

6,000 metal rabbets at $0.08 each - $480

50 fume boards at $9.00 - $450

1 bee blower (optional) at $325 each - $250

75 gallons paint at $16-21 per gallon - $1,500

1 staple gun and compressor - $500

Bees 1,000 packages @ $25.00 - $25,000

Total - $113,100

Honey Handling Equipment

Automatic uncapper - $1,700-$3,000

Frame conveyor - $600

Conveyor drip pan - $250

Cappings melter - $1,000-2,000

Extractor - $1,900-7,800

Settling tanks (each) - $170-250

Spin float (replaces melter) - $3,300

Honey sump - $325-800

Honey pump - $170-190

Flash heater (optional) - $1,000

Barrels (each) - new: $16; used: $8

Barrel truck - $160-250

Hand truck - $125-525

Glass jars (if not selling bulk honey) - $17,300

Bottling equipment (if not selling bulk honey) - $940

Total - $28,948

Vehicles

Flat bed trucks (each) - $1600-1800

Bee booms (each) (mounted) - $2,500

Forklifts (each) - new:$16,000-18,000;used: $8,000-10,000

Pickups - $14,000

Warehouse - $6,000

Land at $3,000/acre 20,000

Rent (house and shop/year) - $15,000-17,000

Labor

Self _ - $30,000
Help, full time, each - $20,000

Help, part time, each - $1,630

Overhead

Utilities (year) - $2,400

Insurance varies

Workman's compensation, health insurance - $13,000

As you can see, when compared to other businesses, starting a commercial beekeeping operation is very reasonable in terms of costs. Also, you don't have to start out with 1,000 colonies either. You can always start small with only a few colonies to see if beekeeping is for you. Keep in mind that a single colony of bees will produce between 50-100 pounds of honey a year! Imagine having up to 100 colonies, then you could sell your local honey at farmer's markets or through a local, natural foods market. Starting small and deciding how large you want to eventually grow your colony is your best bet. That way you know how many colonies you can comfortably manage while becoming more experienced and finding profitable avenues in which to sell your product.

Additional Income: Beeswax Products

What is Beeswax?

Beeswax is produced when honey bees make honey and is produced by the female worker bees who secrete wax from glands on their bellies when they are making honey. The wax is what makes up the hexagon shape structure that encloses the honey. When the worker bees are done filling each hexagon shaped hole with honey, they then use wax to "cap" the honey inside. When honey is harvested, the cap must be removed in order to get the honey out of the honeycomb.

Beeswax is used in many skin care products including lip balms, hand creams, moisturizers, and hand lotions. It is also used in cosmetics, wood waxes, wood finishes, dental molds, leather polishes, and waterproofing supplies. The melting point of wax is around 145 degrees F. When heating wax, be sure to only use a double boiler because it can be very flammable. At 100 degrees F, the wax will be pliable and able to be molded.

Propolis is what bees use to attach the honeycomb walls to each other. Propolis is produced from resins and oils from the plants and pine trees around their environment. The beeswax must be melted and filtered prior to using as an ingredient to anything.

The color of the beeswax is dependent on the plants or trees that the bees made the wax from; colors range from gold or yellow to orange or brown. Beeswax is ideal for candle making due to their clean burn, if done correctly, beeswax candles burn without smoke, dripping hot wax, and produce a very brilliant flame. When the candle is burning the smell emanating is a natural and pleasant scent, the aroma is light, flowery, and sweet.

Benefits of Beeswax in Skin Care

Beeswax can be expensive which is not so great for those who love natural skin care products, but it is great for a beekeeping operator. Why is beeswax so expensive?

- Bees have to fly up to 150,000 miles to produce just one pound of beeswax
- For every one pound of beeswax made, a honey bee has to eat six pounds of honey

- For every 100 pounds of honey harvested, only one to two pounds of wax is produced.

- Beeswax is highly concentrated, so it can be used in small amounts, providing dozens of nutrients and health benefits

Beeswax, when added to skin care or used in place of other waxes or oils, has several beneficial offerings. For example, when added to cold face cream or body cream, beeswax provides a natural protectant because of its inherent ability to shield the skin and block harmful microscopic debris from adhering to your skin. While blocking harmful irritants, your skin is also able to breath and remains moisturized.

The Mayo Clinic advises using a lip balm that is primarily made from beeswax during the winter to treat chapped lips because it is the best natural healing ointment for lips. Choosing skin care products that use beeswax instead of other oils is ideal. These products are typically natural and free of chemicals. Beeswax is also a great option for those who have sensitive skin and get allergies from other skin care products.

Melting beeswax and adding it to your body lotions produces thicker, better hydrating coverage. Beeswax is naturally antibacterial, anti-viral, and anti-inflammatory. If you add beeswax to your body lotion, not only is your skin hydrated, but the health benefits of the beeswax allow your body lotion to help heal minor cuts or abrasions on the surface of your skin. It has been tested and approved for use on minor bacterial infections, and effective at treating diapers rash. You can also apply pure beeswax to your skin by letting it warm in your hands, then molding it wherever you want to apply it. For an undiluted application, organic beeswax is recommended.

As previously mentioned, beeswax is ultra hydrating. When added to body lotions, the beeswax actually draws water from your body to your skin, keeping it consistently moisturized while creating a barrier to lock the moisture in. Beeswax can also be used to aid rough skin because it acts as an emollient and humectant. Emollients have the properties of soothing and softening skin while humectants lock is moisture.

In addition to the hydrating component, beeswax also contains vitamin A, which aids in rehydrating skin and promoting new cell growth. Smoother, softer skin is just days away for those who use beeswax, instead of weeks like some other products. When a product increases cell growth, dead skin sloughs off and new cells are quickly produced, which ends up speeding the process up better than products that don't contain beeswax.

If you forget to apply your beeswax insect repellant before you leave the house, never fear, beeswax can help treat insect bites as well. Not only does it help with wound healing, but also prevents the bites from itching. You can use to beeswax to prevent itching with poison oak and poison ivy as well.

Thomas Thatcher

Do you want perfect, red carpet worthy hair? Or do you just want a natural hair product that you can use every day? Some of Hollywood's best hairstyles are achieved with the use of beeswax. Beeswax is great for keeping your hair right where you want it while smoothing and moisturizing, instead of drying it out. If you are losing hair or trying to grow your hair out, using beeswax helps promote hair growth. Beeswax also has the potential to help your hair grow faster and prevent hair from falling out.

In additional to all these applications, beeswax can be used in the following ways:

- prevent rust from occurring
- natural cheese rinds for cheese makers
- waxing thread for hand sewn leather and creating jewelry
- prevents wood from splitting when hammering in nails
- lubricant for doors, especially helpful for sticking sliding glass doors
- crayon making
- soap
- waterproofing shoes
- shoe polish
- use in place of oil or butter to grease cookie sheets
- candle making
- polish for furniture
- polish for granite countertops
- instead of foil or plastic wrap, you can coat a thin kitchen towel in beeswax and place over leftovers in the refrigerator. When the wax cools it molds to the container

- modeling clay
- wooden spoon or spatula polish
- prevents oxidation of silver, bronze, and copper

There are so many uses and benefits of beekeeping besides making honey. Beekeeping can be a great source of additional income. Quality but reasonably priced products in skin care and personal hygiene are becoming more and more popular; in the last decade natural and organic beauty products have increased in sales tremendously. If you are not interested in actually making the above products, think about selling your wax in bulk, many soap companies, candle makers, etc, would love to have a local natural source for wax.

If you are interested in learning how to make some of these products yourself, a few recipes are included to get you started. These are manageable for beginners and great products you could market and sell.

Recipes

Vitamin E Body Cream

½ cup coconut oil

1 TBSP beeswax

¼ cup of water

10 drops of Vitamin E oil

10 drops of Lavender or Lemon oil

Always use a double boiler when melting beeswax. Melt the coconut oil and beeswax together on a double boiler, once combined add water and remove from heat. Add your Vitamin E oil and essential oil and mix until the wax cools. Before the wax hardens, pour into a tin container or glass jar for easy use when hardened.

Anti-Septic Ointment

¼ cup of beeswax

1/3 cup almond oil (you can also use coconut oil)

1 TBSP jojoba oil (not an essential oil)

20 drops of frankincense essential oil

20 drops of tea tree essential oil

20 drops of lemon essential oil

Heat the almond oil and jojoba oil in a sauce pan on a double boiler. Add the beeswax and remove from heat. If you want to make a hardened balm ointment, add more beeswax to make it thicker. If you want an ointment that is more like the consistency of lip balm or vasoline, add more almond (or coconut) oil. Let the mixture cool slightly before judging whether the mixture is thick/thin enough. Always start with 1 part beeswax with 2 parts oil.

You can add canola oil to the above recipe and use coconut oil in place of the almond oil and create a healing essential salve with 40 drops of any essential oil you want. Essential oils have great healing benefits, which complement the health benefits of beewax.

Itch Relief Salve

2 cups of sweet olive oil

¼ cup of beeswax

1 tsp of chickweed powder

1 TBSP of comfrey powder

On a double burner, mix the sweet olive oil, chickweed powder, and comfrey powder and simmer for 3 hours. Strain the mixture, then add the beeswax and let cool; pour into container, either glass or tin, before the mixture hardens. This salve is excellent for poison ivy or poison oak.

Soothing Analgesic Balm (for pain relief)

1 TBSP chickweed powder

1 TBSP wormwood powder

10 drops of tea tree oil

6 drops of eucalyptus oil

10 drops of lavender oil

4 cups of sweet olive oil

1/3 cup of beeswax

Mix the chickweed powder and wormwood powder together and add to sweet olive oil. Simmer in a saucepan, placed on a double burner, for 3 hours. Remove from heat and add the essential oils and beeswax.

Wood Conditioner

1 TBSP of beeswax

2 cups of turpentine

2 cups of water

1 TBSP of soap flakes (preferably Ivory, Dove, or anything unscented)

Use a cheese grater and shave thin pieces of beeswax into turpentine then place in warm spot outside. Shake the mixture every once in a while until the beeswax melts into the turpentine. Bring two cups of water to a boil and add the soap flakes. Stir this mixture until the soap is dissolved. Combine the water and soap mixture with the beeswax and turpentine mixture and stir quickly to create an emulsion.

Basic Beeswax Candles

This recipe will make 20 ounces of wax, which can make 20 tea tree lights, 5 candles in 4 ounce containers, 2 candles in 10 ounce containers, etc. You can choose what kind of containers and how large you want your candles to be; you can also double this recipe, triple this recipe, etc, for the amount of wax you need for your project.

¾ pound of beeswax

½ cup of coconut oil

10 inches of cotton wick string (do not use string with any metal attached to it)

wick clip (this is optional, it helps keep the wick in place when the candle has melted all the way down until there is little wax left)

candle jars (as many as you want)

double boiler

thermometer

pencils (as many pencils as candle jars)

scissors

Cut your cotton wick string about two inches longer than the height of the candle jar or container, and tie one end of the string in the center of your pencil. Place your pencil on top of the container letting the string dangle down in the middle of the empty container.

Next, heat your beeswax in a sauce pan using a double boiler using low heat. Once the beeswax is melted, add the coconut oil and stir the mixture until completely combined. You want the mixture to reach approximately between 160-165 degrees F.

Pour a thin layer of the mixture in the bottom of each container, making sure that the mixture coats some of the wick as well. Using your fingers (make sure the mixture has cooled enough to touch) place the wick in the center of the container and pull the string so that the wick dries straight. The thin layer of wax should harden in 1 minute.

Next, pour the rest of the oil and beeswax mixture into full the container to the level of your choice, checking to make sure the wick is straight. If you need to adjust the wick, do so while the mixture is still pliable.

Let the candle harden for 24 hours. Then clip the extra length of your wick on top of the candle, to about ¼ of an inch from the top of the wax. Then wait another 24 hours before using your candle for the first time.

When you light your candles, place the flame at the base of the wick, allowing the top of the wax connected to the wick, to melt. Make sure when you use your candles that you let them burn long enough so that the wax runs off to the side of the container. If the center of the candle is only lit for a little while, then the wax in the center will be the only area that melts. This ends up producing a tunnel through the center of your candle, and you definitely want to avoid that!

Nourishing Honey and Beeswax Body Soap

Ingredients

13.5 ounces of olive oil

13.5 ounces of coconut oil

13.5 ounces of beef tallow (fat)

2.4 ounces of castor oil

4.4 ounces of almond oil

1 ounce of beeswax

6.8 ounces of lye (5% discount/superfat)

14.5 ounces of water

1.5 – 2 ounces of honey

2 ounces of your favorite essential oil (caution: make sure the essential oil does not affect "trace"; trace is the point at which the soap mixture becomes a viable and stable emulsion and the lye and oil will no longer separate.)

Supplies:

Electric Emulsion Mixture

Thermometer

Double boiler

Begin by heating your oils and adding your beeswax to melt into the oils. Use your thermometer to raise the oil temperature to 145 degrees F (the temperature at which beeswax melts) and then add your beeswax. Stir the mixture until all the beeswax has melted, and immediately remove from the heat.

Your mixture needs to cool to about 120 degrees F, you can either wait for the mixture to cool by itself, or you can set up a cool water bath to place your pot in after removing from the heat. The borders of the wax inside of the pot will start to harden; to prevent the wax from hardening, continue to stir the mixture until it has cooled to 120 degrees F. Remember to use your thermometer to gauge the correct temperature.

Next, add the honey (prior to the lye) to the oil and beeswax mixture by first taking a small amount of your beeswax and honey mixture and placing in a small bowl. Add the honey and use your stick/emulsion blender to combine the honey, oil, and beeswax. Honey is water based, so it is not going to perfectly combine and mix with the oil and beeswax mixture, so do not get discouraged if you notice some honey that is not blending. Add the honey, oil, and beeswax mixture back into the pot with the rest of the beeswax and oil. Blend this mixture very well.

You are working with two ingredients that do not get along very well, even though they are both produced by honey bees! The honey wants to separate from the oil while the beeswax wants to harden. If the beeswax hardens prior to the lye being added, your soap will come out without the correct balance of ingredients properly distributed.

Next step is to add the lye. Once you add the lye you are going to need to move quickly pouring your soap into their molds. The lye is what is going to make the mixture harden almost instantaneously, without even using your stick/emulsion blender. Again, make sure all ingredients are thoroughly mixed before adding the lye.

Add the lye and stir for about 1-2 minutes. Then add your essential oils to the mixture and use the stick/emulsion blender by placing the mixture and doing 3 shorts blasts of the mixer. The whole process from adding the lye to pouring your mixture into the molds will take about 2 minutes at the most.

Using honey in your soap mixture is going to produce something called "super hot honey gel". What happens is the combination of the honey and beeswax causes the bar to heat up independent of any heat source. The soap can reach upwards up 200 degrees F, so do not touch the soap while it is in the hardening stages.

Allow the soap to rest overnight, for at least 12 hours. After that, you can remove the soap from the molds and cut the soap down to any size you wish.

Additional Income Comes in Many Forms

As you can see, beekeeping has the potential of contributing to additional sources of income aside from honey production. There are so many benefits derived from beeswax and honey and so many ways to use these two ingredients.

Chapter 7

Some Extra Advice

Keep a Healthy Hive

Beekeeping chores have no break. You will have to work with your bees on a daily basis all year long. Only the time duration and intensity of the chores varies from season to season. For example, in winter, there will hardly be an activity so your work will be just to check if your bees are alive and healthy and also that the hives are in good condition. However, during spring and summer, the bees will be very active; foraging pollen and nectar. At this time, you will have a lot of work. Besides inspecting the hives and keeping the bees healthy, you will also have to collect honey; nectar and any other bee product that you plan to sell or use. The busiest times of the year will be spring and fall, just before winter starts, when you need to prepare the bees and the hive for the cold weather.

A beekeeper has to constantly inspect his hives and make sure his bees are hale and hearty. When you examine the frames of your hives, you will be looking for the queen to see if she is laying eggs. You will then check the eggs. You will then check the storage space in the hive to see if the bees have enough nectar, food. Then you will make sure that they have the necessary medication, ventilation, swarm control measures and so on.

You will also need to take precautions against parasites, pesticides, predators and diseases. You will need to medicate the hives with antibiotics and miticides at least twice a year, preferably in spring and fall. You can put up physical barriers such as barbed wire to prevent predators from attacking the hives.

Bee Stings

Honeybees are usually harmless insects that do not unnecessarily harm anybody. The only time they sting is when they feel that their hive is being threatened. However, being a beekeeper and working with a large number of bees is bound to lead a sting at some point of time. Most people only have mild reactions to bee stings. The sting site swells up, feels itchy and turns red. However, there is a small portion of the human population that has a fatal allergic reaction to bee stings. These people need to stay far away from beekeeping and bees in general. However, seasoned beekeepers say that they develop immunity to the bee stings over a period of time because they are stung so often that the body does not consider it a threat anymore. There are a number of ways through which you can reduce the possibility of you getting stung.

Thomas Thatcher

The most important thing to prevent bee stings is to use the right beekeeping gear and use it correctly. You need to make sure that your veil is completely zipped up and that your gloves cover your hand fully. If you wear a full body suit, you need to make sure that all the zips are zipped up properly and that there is no gap for the bee to fly into.

Before you begin any work with the hive, make sure to have your smoker going. First, send in one or two puffs from the bottom of the hive. Then, let out few more puffs from the top. However, make sure that you do not over smoke your bees or else they could die. Once you are sure that the bees are sufficiently knocked out you can work on the hive.

Another useful tip about inspecting hives is to inspect them when the sun is out and shining. The bees will mostly be out foraging. This will allow you access to the hive with hardly any bees in it. Also, make sure that you take your time while inspecting hives. Any movement you make has to be gentle not rushed and in a frenzy. This will get the bees all worked up. Try to avoid swatting since bees see this as a sign of attack and will swarm towards you. Try to get a good grip on the frames so that you do not drop the hives. You should also avoid moving the hive around since this disturbs the equilibrium of the bees. Wear clean clothes since bees seem to hate foul odors. They also do not prefer dark colors, so wear light colored clothes. Also, do not keep honey or sugar anywhere near the hives. This will drive the bees crazy and they will go into a feeding frenzy.

If you do get stung by a bee, remove the stinger immediately. This will prevent the venom from entering your skin. The stinger does not always remain lodged in the skin, but if it does the best way to remove it is to scrape it out with the edge of a credit card. Using tweezers is not advised because squeezing it could release even more venom. Bee stingers emit pheromones that attract other bees to the same or nearby site. So, if you want to prevent further stings, puff smoke onto the sting site to mask the smell. Wash the area and put an ice pack to help with the redness and swelling. If by chance you are stung in the mouth, this can be soothed with a cool drink or even an ice pop. Antihistamines can also be used to reduce the swelling. If you get stung on your throat or mouth and find it difficult to breathe because of the swelling, call emergency services immediately. If you want to be on the safe side, you can carry around an EpiPen for emergencies. There are several signs and symptoms of a more serious allergic reaction. These are not common but include the following: difficulty breathing, feeling faint, feeling dizzy, hives, and swelling of the tongue. If someone in your household is allergic to bee stings and prone to an anaphylactic reaction, he or she should always have their emergency epinephrine readily available and up to date. (Like all medicine, it does expire and lose its effectiveness.) Even after an injection of epinephrine that has reduced symptoms of the reaction, the person who had the reaction should still be taken to the hospital.

The African Honey Bee

The African honey bee can be dangerous to you, your hive, colonies, and environment. This is a very important pest to be aware of and know how to determine if your hive has been infiltrated or is prone to African honey bees moving into the hive.

Originally from Africa, the African honey bee, also known as the "killer bee", is slightly smaller than the standard honey bee, however, it is very difficult to tell with the naked eye. This particular species is actually a hybrid of one of the several species of European Honey Bees combined with the African honey bee. It is covered in fuzz and has modest black stripes on its body, not at dark black as hornets or wasps. Their eyes are large and bulbous; ultra violet rays can be detected with their large eyes, which means they can see in the dark and travel at night.

Although similar in appearance, our standard honey bees, and African honey bees are very different in behavior. African honey bees are very aggressive, attacking randomly, very quickly and in large groups. As mentioned in a previous section, the sting of an African honey bee and a standard honey bee is the same, and both die shortly after their stinger is used.

African honey bees are extremely adaptive and frequently use swarming to establish new hives. They do not store a significant amount of honey due to their consistent traveling behavior. African honey bees frequently move and set up new hives. Since this species is highly adaptive, they have learned to survive on limited food and water, being able to survive for longer periods of time than their counterparts, the standard honey bee. When resources for food and water are depleted, the colony will immediately move to find another nest to live in; they do not participate in the "winter cluster" nearly as much as standard honey bees.

When the African honey bees move to a new location, where their nest is located is not important; they will live almost anywhere, and begin to exploit the environment right away. Because they are so highly aggressive and defensive, when African honey bees move into a new territory, they compete for the food that the standard honey bees depend on to make their honey. The African honey bee is faster and more competitive, as a result, the standard honey bee has less and less access to food and resources, their colony begins to dwindle, and eventually whole colonies will die out.

In additional to their aggressive behavior towards other bees and competing for food, African honey bees are known for their aggression towards humans as well. When you have a colony set up and African honey bees move in and take over, you have to remove them immediately and safely. It is probably best to call your local pest control company and do not attempt to remove it on your own if you are not experienced. Most of the time African honey bees are disturbed due to lawn mowers, tractors, weed eaters, any kind of loud electric equipment. They can sense a threat from up to 50 feet away and can sense vibrations of motorized equipment from 100 feet away. African honey bees respond faster to threats, a larger number in the swarm, resulting in more stings, ten times more than the standard honey bee. Once they sense a threat and begin to chase their victim, they are known to travel up to a quarter of a mile in pursuit.

These pests also have different genes than the standard honey bee, resulting in different presentations and symptoms of mites, fungi, and bacteria. If you are unable to spot an African honey bee that is presenting with a potential disease or pest, there is a likelihood that your colony could become infected.

There are several ways the beekeeping industry is responding to the threat of the African honey bee migrating to the United States. First, beekeepers are controlling the African honey bee through "drone-flooding". This term refers to large quantities of standard honey bees were queen bees are commercially being bred. Having a large quantity of drone honey bees surrounding the area where queens are mating, limits the possibility of queen bees mating with African honey bees. The greatest deterrent is a large, healthy, well established colony of standard honey bees. Sickness and population decline of the standard honey bee allows additional resources to go unused, more food is available, and African honey bees end up relocating.

Another method beekeepers use to keep African honey bees managed, is frequent "re-queening", which means the queen is replaced quite often. This ensures that the queen continues to be the standard honey bee species, and continues to mate with the standard honey bee drones.

Lastly, beekeepers have started exterminating wild bee nests, resulting in more standard honey bee colonies.

Conclusion

We have reached the end of this book. I hope you liked it and I hope it helps you gain a lot from beekeeping. Take it one step at a time and do not be discouraged by a bee sting or two. It is an occupational hazard, but trust me; the benefits are numerous. I hope you enjoyed learning as much as I enjoyed teaching.

Thank you for reading this book and good luck!

Beekeeping

Thomas Thatcher

Beekeeping

Thomas Thatcher

Made in the USA
Lexington, KY
06 December 2017